THE SCIENCE OF WRITING

Michael Mamah

ISBN: 978-1512106176

DEDICATION

To my wife Kati,
My three children Lizi, Vicky and Mikey,
My nieces Caroline and Sophie,
My parents Judith and Okpoma,
My brother and sisters Tonye, Ebinimi, Marika and Terike,
My grandparents Nagymami, Nagyapa, Opumama and
Opupapa,
My uncle and aunts; Aci Néni, Potyi Néni, Bori Néni,
Berci Bácsi, Comfort, Dorcas, Ivotari
and to Peter Bartók.

CONTENTS

1

DIALOGUE

Contents:

Preview

We start with the very important topic of writing dialogue. Before we start, please read these two passages. After Passage 1, pause for five seconds, and then read Passage 2.

Passage 1

A pretty young lady, Angela, walked into the room and was greeted by a middle-aged gentleman named Steve.

"Hi Angela," said Steve. "Hi," said Angela. "How was your trip?" asked Steve.

"Oh, it was nice," said Angela.

Steve gave Angela a big hug. "Oh! I missed you," said Angela.

"Me too," said Steve. "When are the others coming?" asked Angela.

"They will be here soon," replied Steve.

PAUSE FOR FIVE SECONDS!!!!

Passage 2

A pretty young lady, Angela, walked into the room and was greeted by a middle-aged gentleman named Steve.

"Hi Angela," smiled Steve, cheerfully.

"Hi," replied Angela, closing the door behind her.

"How was your trip?" asked Steve, reaching for her coat.

"It was nice," grinned Angela, handing her coat to him.

Steve placed the coat on a hanger and gave Angela a big hug.

"Oh! I missed you," he sighed, squeezing her tight. "Me too," mumbled Angela, stroking his hair.

Angela looked into Steve's deep brown eyes curiously, "When are the others coming?"

Steve hesitated, then put on his shades composing himself. "They will be here soon."

Which passage did you prefer? Though the topic was the same in both passages, Passage 2 was much better. Do you know what made the difference?

The dialogue—which is what this chapter is all about! When you write a book, usually a story—it could be a true story or it could be fiction. Either way there will be dialogue in it.

As you can see, the style you use to write the dialogue leaves a deep impact on the reader and usually makes a big difference in the quality of the book.

Structure

For dialogue to be clearly defined, you must follow a basic format. There are five essential points you have to keep in mind for effective dialogue-writing:

1. Use double quotations.

2. Start the dialogue using a capital letter.

3. End the dialogue with a comma before closing the double quotation.

4. The "said" following the dialogue must be in small letters.

5. All the statements of the dialogue must be on separate lines and indented for effect.

Consider the following example:

> "I am going to the shop," said Sharon.

1. "… ," is the dialogue

> "I am going to the shop,"…

is in double quotations.

2. The dialogue starts with a capital letter. The "I" in

> "I am going to the shop,"…

3. There is a comma after the dialogue.

> "I am going to the shop,"…

4. The "said" following the dialogue is in small letters.

> "I am going to the shop," said Sharon.

5. And finally, all of the above is indented and on

separate lines.

That is:

"I am going to the shop," said Sharon.

Types of Dialogue

Dialogue can be divided into Simple and Advanced.

A. Simple

This can be further classified into two types:

1. Simple Basic
2. Simple Emotion

1. Simple Basic

It is easy to recognize simple basic dialogue as the reported speech is followed by words such as:

said, answered, replied.

For example:

"I am going to the shop," said Sharon.
"Okay. Don't be late," answered Paul.

2. Simple Emotion

Here, words such as "croaked" and "screamed" convey the emotion of the character, and besides providing some variation in the writing, prevents it from becoming too monotonous as we saw in Passage 1 above. Using simple emotion for writing dialogue highlights the feelings of the character and often transfers the emotion from the book to the reader.

For example:

> "Okay," Stephen croaked.
> "Get out of my house!" screamed Tina.
> "Be quiet!" she whispered.

B. Advanced

When you write advanced dialogue, you combine a few features. These features can be divided into three parts:

1. Action
2. Feeling
3. Combination

1. Action

In action, you use verbs to describe what the character did followed by the dialogue without using any of the "simple" dialogue words such as "said," "replied, "answered," and so on.

For example:

> Amanda stroked his hair. "I am getting really fond of you."

2. Feeling:

This is similar to the action described above, but the words you use will help you see the emotion the character is going through followed by the dialogue, again without using any of the "simple" dialogue words such as "said."

For example:

> Angela was getting frightened, "Is there a light in this room?"

The words you choose to write the dialogue will either convey direct action or a description of the action.

For example:

> Sebastian looked strangely unnerved, "A wildebeest?"

> Stephen's pride was totally shattered, "You kissed him?"

3. Combination

You can combine the dialogue described in

"Advanced," that is, "Action" and "Feeling," and also with "Basic" dialogue types using different combinations for a variety of scenarios.

Here are some examples:

i.   Basic combined with action:

"I missed you," she said, fondling his toes.

ii. Combined action of one character with the action of another:

"This way, Mr. Stephens," she glanced at the porter, who hurriedly opened the door.

iii. Action combined with another action and then another.

"I will make sure you have the time of your life," Jenny smiled warmly and lowered her voice, leaning closer.

iv. Combination of a description and a feeling.

The handcuffs cut through his flesh; he could take no more punishment, "Okay, I'll tell you where he is hiding."

You can let your imagination loose on the different types of combinations that would fit your story.

Dialogue Positions

Dialogues could be before, after, or sandwiched. Let us look at some examples:

1. Before

This is the most common type of dialogue.

For example:

"Hurry home," she begged.

2. After

For example:

Jason was impressed, "You are a surgeon and you write books?"

3. Sandwiched

For example:

"Sarah, come in," he smiled. "I'll show you around."

Now start writing first using each of the simple dialogue types I described earlier and then do some combinations. Have fun.

MICHAEL MAMAH

2

INNER DIALOGUE

Contents:

Preview

In the previous chapter, we learned how to write effective dialogue. Now we are going to learn to convey emotion or inner dialogue. Before we start, please read these two passages. After Passage 1, pause for five seconds and then read Passage 2.

Passage 1

James sensed he knew her... trusted her, But how? Why? Thought James.

He remembered the document she wrote. R? Thought James. As in Rebecca? Thought James. Is that the love of my live? He thought.

He closed his eyes, trying to rekindle memories of the beautiful holiday in Tuscana. Was it an accident? Nothing. A total blank. Think. He thought.

There was only darkness. He saw his clothes on a table nearby, folded inside a clear plastic bag. They were covered in confetti. My God! It must have been a crazy night, thought James.

Now James rotated his head very slowly. I'm in Long Island!? Thought James. James Peterside's head throbbed. He was now seated upright in his bed.

PAUSE FOR FIVE SECONDS!!!

Passage 2

James sensed he knew her…trusted her. *But how? Why?*

He remembered the document she wrote. *R?* James thought, uncertain. *As in…Rebecca? Is that….the love of my life?*

He closed his eyes, trying to rekindle memories of the beautiful holiday in Tuscana. Nothing. A total blank. *Think.* Only darkness.

He saw his clothes on a table nearby, folded inside a clear plastic bag. They were covered in confetti. *My God! It must have been a crazy night.* Now James rotated his head very slowly. *I'm in Long Island!?* James Peterside's head throbbed. He was now seated upright in his bed.

Passage 2 is clearly better. What is it that makes Passage 2 better? Let's take a closer look at the techniques in writing inner dialogue.

Structure

There is a format in writing inner dialogue, just like the format in writing dialogue. You have to keep in mind the following five points when writing inner dialogue:

1. The inner dialogue that is described is in italics.

2. The description of the emotion starts with a capital letter.

3. A punctuation ends the description of the emotion.

4. The thought is in small letters following the emotion (if there is a comma after the emotion).

5. All of the above are on separate lines and indented.

An example is:

> *He does not look like he's twenty years old*, thought Sharon.

1. The description of the emotion is in italics.

> *He does not look like he's twenty years old*,

2. The inner dialogue starts with a capital letter. The H in

> *He does not look like he's twenty years old*,

3. There is a comma after the inner dialogue (or other punctuation).

> *He does not look like he's twenty years old*,

4. The action (in this case, the word "thought") following the dialogue is in small letters.

> *He does not look like he's twenty years old*, thought Sharon.

5. And finally, all of the above is indented and on separate lines. That is:

> *He does not look like he's twenty years old*, thought

Sharon.

Types of Inner Dialogue

Inner dialogue can be divided into Simple and Advanced.

A. Simple

Common examples of simple inner dialogue are:

> thought Sharon, he thought, she thought, he wondered

For example:

> *He does not look like he's twenty years old*, thought Sharon.

> *I think she has caught on to me*, he thought.

B. Advanced

When you write advanced inner dialogue, you combine a few features. These features can be divided into three parts.

1. Action
2. Feeling
3. Combination

1. Action

Action uses verbs to describe what the character did followed by the inner dialogue, without writing said, or any of the other "simple" inner dialogue type words.

For example:

> Amanda opened the door. *It is really dark in here.*

It can also be written after the character has done the action.

> *I'm in Paris!?* Stephen's head throbbed.

2. Feeling

Feeling is similar to action above but here inner dialogue of the character is depicted followed by the emotion, again, without any of the "simple" words like thought, wondered, and so on.

For example:

> Jason felt like he had awoken inside a Steven King movie. *What is this place?*

> Angela sensed she knew him … trusted him. *But how? Why?*

You can use words to make the feeling or the action

direct or you can describe it.

For example:

> Sebastian's hands were trembling. *I think someone left the cage unlocked.*
>
> Stephen's pride took a huge beating. *I can't believe she kissed him.*

3. Combination

The above "advanced" type inner dialogues can be combined with one another or with basic inner dialogue types.

Here are some examples:

i. Basic combined with action:

> *I like him,* she thought, fondling his toes.

ii. Action of one character combined with the action of another.

> *I'm in Paris?* Jane's head throbbed; she reached for the chair as she was feeling faint.

iii. Action combined with another action and then another.

> *I am going to have the time of my life.* Jenny smiled

warmly and lowered her voice, leaning closer.

iv. Combination of a description and a feeling.

> The handcuffs cut through his flesh; he could take no more punishment. *I better start talking or my hands will fall off.*

You can let your imagination loose on the different types of combinations that would enhance your story.

4. Advanced Level 2 with Simile

Here the character's thoughts are described using a simile. Let's take a look at an example:

> He looked at his bank account in despair—despite making a lot of money he had trouble maintaining it… like water, money seemed to slip through his fingers alarmingly fast.
> *At this rate I will never be able to repay my debt.*

Here you can see that the character "thinks" the thought, that is (At this rate I will never be able to pay my debt) and then there is a simile (like water pouring through his hands) telling you how hard it is for him to keep his money.

Inner Dialogue Positions

Inner Dialogue could be before, after, or sandwiched.

Let us look at some examples:

1.   Before

Here the inner dialogue is before the sentence. For example:

> *Martin,* he thought, picturing the sinewy, bald bounty hunter.

2. After

For example:

> Jason was impressed. *He must be a genius.*

3. Sandwiched

Here the inner dialogue is sandwiched between the phrase.

For example:

> He closed his eyes, trying to remember an accident. Nothing. A total blank. *Think.* Only darkness.

It could be a reverse sandwich, or multiple-layered sandwich.

For example:

> *R?* James thought, uncertain. *As in …Rebecca? Is that….the love of my life?*

Now start writing first using each of the simple inner dialogue types described earlier—then do some combinations. Have fun.

3

ACTION

Contents:

Preview

Again, in order to give you a hand in your quest at becoming a good writer and to encourage you, I will demonstrate a raw example and a tweaked up example of writing—a before and after version of writing.

Raw Examples

1. The movement gave him a headache
2. He looked back to the room
3. David became afraid

Tweaked Up Examples

1. The movement sent a spike of pain radiating through his skull
2. He turned his gaze back toward the room
3. David was overcome by a sudden, instinctive sense of danger… not just for himself… but for everyone.

Structure

There is a format in writing action and it is simple. When you write an action, unlike dialogue or inner dialogue, you just write it in normal text.

For example:

> The blonde lady put a finger to her lips.

> Or

> Dr. Andrews quickly placed a firm hand on Jason's sternum.

Simple, isn't it.

Classification

Writing action can be classified into simple and advanced.

A. Simple

Here you can write simply what the character does. For example:

> Stephen gazed at her

> John reached for his hat

> David tried to move his hand

B. Advanced

As we have read from the previous chapters and if you

were vigilant you may have also noticed that the action part of writing is a sort of bridge between the other parts, that is, between dialogue, character description, and scene description. In the advanced version of the other parts of writing, there is always an action part as will be explained below.

This is a perfect opportunity for me to emphasize the fact that, as with any other science, writing also has classifications. The objective of classification is to help study material. A subject like writing or even anatomy of the body has too much information to be processed by the working memory in one attempt, which is why we break it down to easily analyze and digest the subject. By breaking up a topic into subtopics, it does not mean that the sub-topics are separate, independent entities. Action is just one of the parts of writing that interconnects the different parts as we will see in the following examples.

We can see that the advanced parts of the action discussion can be classified according to the part of writing it is combined with. Let's take a look at some examples:

1. In Combination with Dialogue

a. Amanda stroked his hair. "I am getting really fond of you."

b. "This way, Mr. Stephens," she glanced at the porter, who hurriedly opened the door.

c. "I will make sure you have the time of your life," Jenny smiled warmly and lowered her voice, leaning closer.

This does not mean that every dialogue is an action. An example of a dialogue that is not an action is:

"I am going to the shop," said Sharon.

Technically, you will say this is an action, but for all intents and purposes this statement is classified as dialogue.

2. In Combination with Inner Dialogue

a. Amanda stroked his hair. *I think I'm in love.*

b. Stephen opened the door. *It is really dark in here.*

c. Humphrey kicked the door open. *If I find him with her I will kill them both.*

Again, not all Inner Dialogue descriptions are actions, to take a look at an example:

He does not look like he's twenty years old, thought Sharon.

3. In Combination with Character Description

a. He walked out of the honeymoon suite, his face beaming, "I am king of the world."

b. A powerfully built man effortlessly unstraddled his BMW motorcycle and advanced with the intensity of a panther stalking its prey. His gaze was intense. His head bald with a large black tribal tattoo above his left ear partly covered by the upturned collar of his black leather jacket.

c. A tall delicate lady clumsily climbed out of her red Porsche and staggered with the confusion of a gazelle shot with a tranquilizer gun.

Again, not all character descriptions can be classified as action parts of writing. An example is:

Jane, a small English brunette with a Munchkin voice and the energy of a Chihuahua on Red bull.

The above sentence is clearly a character description that has no element of action in it.

4. In Combination with Scene Description

She walked casually along the sunny street and spotted Andrew at Zsombolyai Street. She turned anxiously into building No. 8. Nervously, she entered the code to let her in. It was an ill-lit hallway with ashen walls and a titian railing behind which was a lift built around 1942 at the time of the Second World War.

Again, not all scene descriptions are action descriptions. Take a look at this example:

Up on the hill in Deepcar stood the four bedroom family home of the Mamahs. A thick blanket of snow covered its roof as steam from Kata cooking breakfast emerged from the open window. Children's toys and clothes lay all around the house; however, despite the mess the house was immaculately clean.

MICHAEL MAMAH

4

CHARACTER DESCRIPTION

Contents:

Introduction

When writing a book, you are telling a story. To do this you need to relay to the reader all that happened, including what the character said, which is the dialogue (we covered dialogue in a previous chapter). You also need to describe the place where the action takes place or the scenery, the actions (all covered in different chapters), and the characters that do all the actions in the book, which will be covered in this chapter.

For the reader to imagine what you are writing and to take them into another world, you need to take care of all these aspects, which is the magic of writing. I have seldom heard anyone say a Hollywood film (with tens of millions even hundreds of million dollar budgets) is better than the book. Almost always people say the book is better. So it is very important to be able to write good character descriptions.

Preview

Raw Example:

Sam was six feet two, with blue eyes and blonde hair.

This is a simple character description and you see

character descriptions like this in novels, but the magic happens when you make it more complicated, more interesting, more artistic, if you will.

Tweaked Up Example:

> Sam was a tall and swarthy young man with long curly blonde hair wearing a silk geeky button-down gigolo shirt with way too many buttons undone.

This second description colors your fantasy and you have a more vivid picture of the character, drawing the reader into a magical world, which is what good writing is all about.

But how is this done? Well, there is a science to it. I have analyzed character description and will relay its architecture to you making what may look like an unachievable task into a scientific write-up that anyone can do once they have mastered the technique.

.

Parts of Character Description

I have divided character descriptions into two parts: Direction and Dynamics.

A. Direction
B. Dynamics

Now let us look at these one by one.

A. Direction

Actually this category can be divided into three forms:

1. Antagonistic
2. Agonistic
3. Neutral

Let us start with the first one:

1. Antagonistic

Antagonistic is when you say something about the character and then say something which is the opposite, thereby moving the fantasy of the reader, keeping them alert and interested. Look at the following example:

> Jane, a small English brunette with a Munchkin voice and the energy of a Chihuahua on Redbull.

We start with a fact:

> 1. Jane, a small English brunette with a Munchkin voice,

Then we go antagonistic, that is, we say the opposite about her.

> 2. and the energy of a Chihuahua on Redbull

This is the first category to give the reader/audience an

emotional, or should I say mental, experience—saying something and then contradicting with the opposite.

2. Agonistic

This is when you say something about a character and then strengthen your point by further highlighting it. Let's take a look at an example:

> Jane, a small English brunette with a Munchkin voice and a freckled face, who could not look anyone in the eye—there was something poignant and childlike about her.

Here we see Jane has a high pitched (Munchkin) voice, she is shy (cannot look anyone in the eye) and is poignant and childish. So each extra word just strengthens our point, which is a description of the word Agonistic.

3. Neutral

This is when you describe a character but without the contraindication or elaborations described earlier. Here is an example:

> She wore a tight yellow dress with a décolletage, large golden earrings dangled from her ears, and her nails were painted bright red.

There is no real direction in this example. It is a neutral description.

B. Dynamics

You will learn the many ways you can word sentences to describe a character. I find this a very useful tool. Using this you can achieve three things: (1) using set out dynamic patterns you can make your own character descriptions, (2) you can analyze other writers by calculating and analyzing the dynamics of their character description, and (3) you can invent your own original character descriptions either based on other writers or completely original ones.

There are several patterns in the dynamics. You can use preset patterns to write your own character descriptions. You can also analyze other writers' patterns and write character descriptions in their style or you can make up your own original patterns and create your own style of writing.

I have written a few examples of patterns on dynamics of character description, but there are many more. You can use these and try to come up with your own examples. Remember the more you write the better writer you will be—to put it simply, practice makes perfect.

1. EaB (External and Antagonistic Behavior)
2. Time Travel
3. Roller Coaster
4. Understatement
5. Exaggerated Finish
6. Body Speech
7. Metamorphosis
8. Comparison to Stars

9. Comparison to Animals

1. EaB or External and Antagonistic Behavior

Example 1a:

Jane, a small English brunette with a Munchkin voice and the energy of a Chihuahua on Redbull,

Here we have the following:

1. External Description (E)
2. Antagonistic Behavioral Description (aB)
Abbreviated: EaB

Take a look at the next example to see a similar EaB dynamic character description:

Example 1b:

Agatha, a dainty tow-headed Polish lass, had a clarion voice and the vivacity of a cocker spaniel on heat,

Again external description followed by an antagonistic behavioral description.

But EaB is not the only type of Dynamics/Architecture. Let us look at a few more.

Some other types of architecture are the following:

2. Time Travel

Example 2a:

His face, normally radiantly smiling, drooped like an aged plum as he sat on the bed.

The dynamics of this is "Time Travel."

From the above example, the picture that emerges is that in the past his face smiled radiantly and now in the "present" his face is sad and gloomy.

Let us look at another example of this type of time travel dynamics

Example 2b:

His face, usually beaming with laughter, was somber like a world with no music.

Again, in the past his face was beaming with laughter but now in the present he is somber.

3. Roller Coaster

The dynamics of this type of character description goes in a wave form. Again, an example will help me explain.

Example 3a:

She towered over her classmates, she was never

mistaken for an adult but was taller than most of her teachers.

This is an antagonistic wave form, in the sense that first,

1. She is taller than her classmates (Wave up)
2. Then she is never mistaken for an adult, that is, she is a child (Wave down)
3. She is taller than most of her teachers (wave up)

And to use the previous type of examples:

Example 3b:

Jane was a petite English brunette—although she had the aggression of a hungry wolf, she was too shy to leave her house without her boyfriend Hank.

So again antagonistic wave forms up and down:

1. She was small (Wave down)
2. She had a lot of energy (Wave up)
3. She is shy and scared (Wave down).

4. Understatement

The dynamics of this type of character description goes on to make a statement and then uses an understatement to emphasize the point.

Let us take a look at some sample sentences using the previous examples.

Example 4a:

Jane is not a giant but to say she is of average height would be an understatement.

Example 4b:

Jane is not a barbaric maniac but to say she is temperamental would be an understatement.

This example speaks for itself. It is a good tool to stimulate the readers' fantasy and to get the reader to imagine what it is that you are writing about which keeps them awake and engaged.

5. Exaggerated Finish

The character is first described and then the last bit is exaggerated.

Example 5a:

She wore a skin tight red mini skirt, a loose blouse, and her long greasy hair hung down covering half her face, urgently needing a wash.

Example 5b:

Andrew was tall and had a loud harsh voice. When he talked to you, you felt he was shouting at you.

6. Body Speech

Here you describe an action or expression and explain

what it "says."

Example 6:

> He walked out of the honeymoon suite, his face beaming "I am king of the world."

Again, the example describes itself but you can say his face "said" I am king of the world.

7. Metamorphosis

Example 7:

> He had a long unshaven face with protruding teeth; he looked like a Photoshop transformation of a horse to a rat paused halfway.

In this example, the character that is being described has characteristics of two different things, a rat and a horse, so metamorphosis stating his face looked like a Photoshop transformation paused half way gives the reader a good image of what you are trying to say.

8. Comparison to Stars

Example 8:

> He was tall and had long Michael Bolton-like hair.

This speaks for itself. We all know stars, so saying his

hair looks like Michael Bolton's or a figure like Liz Taylor's gives you a perfect image of what the writer is saying.

9. Comparison to Animals

Animals have external features but also characters, that is, as slow as a snail, as cunning as a fox. Comparing your character to animals again is a good tool to describe your character.

Example 9:

> You could barely make out his figure in the dark; his eyes glimmered in the moonlight like a black panther hunting for its prey

Try your hand at some of this and I believe you will have great fun trying out this stuff. Soon you will feel it is part of you and like learning a new language it will come to you naturally.

5

SCENE DESCRIPTION

Contents:

The following is a list of scene descriptions:

III. Scene Description Aids
    A. Description Aid
    B. Environmental Aid
    C. History Aid

When you write, the parts listed here can be arranged in any combination and all the parts need not always be present, but the introduction must come first and it can be omitted.

Introduction

When describing a scene, you start with a statement that gives the reader an introduction on what you are going to describe. The statement can be divided into simple or advanced. Let us take a more in-depth look at these.

A. Simple

This could be a single part or a double part.

1. Single Part

For example:

    a. The house was a disaster
    b. The cottage looked cozy
    c. The lodge seemed to be comfortable

2. Double Part

For example:

    a.   It was Melrose Beach House. And Melrose Beach House was in shambles.

    b.   We were in 17 Pen Nook Glade. And Pen Nook Glade was in its usual state.

B. Advanced

Here the introduction can be combined with action, location, or your own theme. Take a look at some examples.

1. Action Introduction

    a.   Our destination was the New York Metropolitan Health Center on Maple Street. It was an ugly slab of concrete surrounded day and night by...

    b.   We were headed for 17 Pen Nook Glade— a 1,700 square feet four bedroom family home.

2. Location Introduction

    a.   At the heart of the skyline, a mountainous pillar of dark glass and silver metalwork rose up, its zenith adorned...

    b.   In the eleventh district in Budapest was a seven story building. It blended....

Parts

In actual fact, the meat of a scene description is this section—the "Parts," where we describe things such as the door was red, the window pane was yellow, and so on. In our analysis and discussion of writing, we will divide parts scene description into simple and advanced.

A. Simple Part Description

1. Level 1

This is a simple part description describing what you see.

> a.　The doors were split and smashed off their hinges.
>
> b.　The walls were dented in the shape of hammers, clubs, and frying pans.
>
> c.　The hotel room had a single bed. No flowers. No carpet.

2. Level 2

Level 2 can be divided into three parts:

i.　Part Description
ii.　Simple Part Character Combo
iii.　Simple Dynamic Part Description

i. Part Description

In part description, the part described is highlighted:

    a.   The ship's stealth-profile was painted gunmetal gray,

    b. its zenith adorned with a golden sphere

    c.   that glinted like a beacon. The Gamara Tower

ii. Simple Part Character Combo

Here the character is connected to the part of the scene described.

For example:

    Jason saw his clothes on a nearby table, folded in a plastic bag and covered in mud.

iii. SimpleDynamicPart Description

In simple, dynamic part description, the parts described are in motion.

For example:

    Cigarette butts and tissue paper floated grimly in the Jacuzzi.

B. Advanced Part Description

This is a multi-step description of the scene where the characters' actions can be intertwined with the scene description.

For example:

> a.   The sofas and dozens of towels lying on the floor of the sunken living room were fetid and discolored with the excreta and the fur of their pet dogs, sheep, and cattle. The sweat of the farmers following the struggles also lingered in the air.
>
> b.   The white carpet had become gray from the constant traffic of cattle and sheep herded in from "The Luange Farm" every night.
>
> c.   He walked through the dark alley and gazed at the silver handle of the locked door.

Scene Description Aids

The scenes can be altered by adding sentences to improve your description. You can use the following three aids to do this:

A. Description Aid
B. Environmental Aid
C. History Aid

A. Description Aid

The description aid usually accompanies the introduction part of a scene description. Let us look at some examples:

> a. The Johnny Walker Pub, a velvet-rope guarded entertainment hotspot
> b. The 347-foot luxury yacht, the "Ocean Climax"

B. Environmental Aid

Here you describe the scene by describing the environment.

For example:

> The Queen Mary Luxury Yacht sailed in. Its mast emerged unhurriedly through the dense fog that rose gently from the dark bays of the Adriatic.

C. History Aid

History explaining the background of the scene or building can come in handy in scene descriptions.

For example:

> a. Mansonni had made architectural history by engineering the skyscraper's massive dome.

b. And now, more than forty hundred years later, the 427-foot-tall structure still stood its ground, an immovable giant, the "Carta De Aguero."

Feel free to try writing your own scene descriptions using the guidelines I have provided.

6

MICROSCOPY

Contents:

We will now talk about microscopy. Microscopy takes an in-depth look at writing. In the previous section, we went through the different parts of writing, which is especially useful for character description. In this section, we will begin by looking at the microscopy of different parts of writing, and then look at the architecture of microscopy, which are the building blocks to assemble your character description.

Microscopy Parts

Anatomy

Here we will give you some examples of various ways used to describe different parts of the body and clothes.

Age
1. In his forties
2. Thirty-something
3. Young

Breasts
1. Silicone breasts
2. Fake breasts
3. Intense breasts

Character
1. Tipsy looking
2. Jock
3. Self-proclaimed nerve

Clothes
1. Casual, loose-fitting blue black suit
2. Overly baggy clothes
3. Cut off white T-shirt
4. Well dressed
5. Puffy pink vest

Complexion

1. Tan
2. Swarthy
3. Well-tanned
4. Olive complexion

Face

1. High cheekbones
2. Handsome chiseled face
3. Porous-face
4. Red drunken face

Eyes

1. Gentle eyes
2. Amber eyes
3. Velvety eyes
4. Aquamarine eyes
5. Arctic blue eyes

Hair

1. Honey butter colored
2. Light ash blonde
3. Rich auburn blonde
4. Deep burgundy
5. Dark mahogany brown

Other

1. Assertive gait
2. Willowy elegance
3. Thoughtful calm

Microscopic Architecture

A character description has different parts.

1. Parts of body.

For example:

body parts like velvety eyes, amber eyes, etc., clothes like cut off white T-shirt, puffy pink vest, etc.

2. Action of part.

What the character does is depicted here.
For example: She now stroked his "bushy hair"

3. Description of part

For example:

His bushy hair, greasy from the tiring hours in the mine….

4. Behavior of part.

For example:

She had peach blonde hair and a warm smile that radiated a pleasant glow from her mischievous face.

The above can be written freely in any combination you

like, giving your character descriptive life.

Thesaurus Levels (of Microscopy)

Let us look at action description from a microscopic point of view.

We can divide the microscopy or should I say in-depth analysis/zoom in to three levels:

Thesaurus Levels 1 to 3

Let us start with Thesaurus Level 1

Thesaurus Level 1

Here the action word (verb) is simply replaced by a complicated word. This is the maximum you can get from a thesaurus online or book. Levels 2 and 3 are where this book comes in handy because that cannot be simply retrieved from your online or published thesaurus. But for now let us look at Level 1.

Raw example
1. Stephen looked at her
2. The girl pulled up to him
3. His muscles tensed
4. She switched off the lights
5. She looked out of the window

Level 1 Thesaurus
1. Stephen gazed at her
2. The girl reached up to him
3. His muscles tightened
4. She turned off the lights
5. She stared out of the window

Thesaurus Level 2

Here one word (verb) is replaced by more.

Raw example
1. John walked to the field
2. He removed a small device from his pocket
3. He looked at the blonde nurse
4. Jason went to the counter
5. David looked at the window

Level 2 Thesaurus
1. John took a step toward the field
2. He readily produced a small device from his pocket
3. He shot a glance at the blonde nurse
4. Jason walked over to the counter
5. Jason stared up at the window

Thesaurus Level 3

Level 3 is when the statement is completely changed only the meaning is the same

Raw

1. But the movement caused his head to hurt.
2. He started shaking very much
3. Very fast
4. He blew up
5. The slim lady lifted her finger to hush him

Level 3 Thesaurus

1. But the movement sent a spike of pain radiating through his skull
2. His entire body started vibrating intensely
3. In a rush of thunder
4. He exploded into a thousand shards
5. The slim lady put a finger to her lips and then

In conclusion, this is a small introduction about writing actions in books. My advice is to practice a lot remembering that you will always become better. Think of the time when you were three years old and had just begun to talk. Your vocabulary was obviously much less advanced than it is today; however, you still continued to talk. You did not say "Hey! I talk like a child and this is unacceptable. I must wait till I am twenty-eight years old when my speech will be developed. Until then I will not say a word." That is obviously not the correct approach. In the same way as a budding writer you should continue to write. Read my book and get a guide and become better and better writing more and more and more.

MICHAEL MAMAH

7

THE STRUCTURE OF THE BOOK

Contents:

Statistics of the Five Parts

Though there is no hard and fast rule, generally, Dialogue is about 25 percent of a book, Inner Dialogue is 5 percent, Action 30 percent, Character Description 25 percent, Scene Description 10 percent, and other (e.g., Narration, etc.) is 5 percent.

Of course, there can be some flexibility in writing the different parts; however, it is a good guide to see how much of each part to write.

Creativity

I attended a singer song writer course in Hollywood, California, and I was lectured by Allan Rich, a song writer for great stars like Whitney Houston and Toni Braxton. He said creativity cannot be taught—if you believe in God, then it comes from God; if you don't believe in God, then it comes from the Universe.

The question is how receptive are you to this "sound" that delivers creativity to you.

There are two reasons for an individual not to be creative:

A. No "Reception"

Here there is no idea; the writer's head is blank. This occurs in writers block also to established writers. However, this is the rarer case. The majority of the non-creativity of individuals is from "interference."

B. Interference

In interference, the writer has an idea but a "negative thought/voice in the head" discourages the writer on his creativity. In this case, the writer starts to write something, and then feels that it is not good, just "rubbish" and stops writing.

The medicine for this type of problem is to just continue to write and then when you have finished to review it and tell yourself that you will correct it in the end. You will be amazed at how impressed you will be about your work and how little you will eventually need to correct.

Plot

I have discussed the parts of writing and also given you hints on writing. The next question is the plot. Well, there are two approaches to writing a plot and they are:

> The Adventure Approach, and
> The Preplanned Approach.

A. The Adventure Approach

In the adventure approach, you start off with a character, for instance, Tom. Now something happens to Tom, for example, Tom goes to the supermarket. At this point you have no idea what will happen to Tom but after writing how he walks to the supermarket you think of what will happen next. Then, say, he meets Anne who steals his bag. You still don't know how it will end but you think of what Tom does, say, Tom runs after Anne but she jumps into a red Porsche and drives off, and so on.

So you make up the story as you go along.

This can have different forms. The story might be 100 percent adventure where you have no clue who the characters are, you just pick, say, Tom and then you continue his journey till you get to page 500 when you wrap up the book and the end will be a twist because even you had no idea how it would end.

You can have some idea of what will happen, say, if you want to write a romantic novel about Jason and Amanda, who are from different backgrounds and first do not like each other but then fall in love. So using these points you can start your adventure.

B. The Preplanned Approach

In this case, you know exactly what you want to write. All you are doing is downloading the story from your brain into the computer/onto paper.

The best way to start this is to make a table of content and then start each chapter and write in detail.

Of course, there is a continuum between The Adventure Approach and The Preplanned Approach, which are two extremes and most books are written somewhere in between them.

Analysis of Writing

In order to develop your writing style, it is often a good idea to analyze the writing patterns of your favorite authors. To do this, I advise you to pick one of the five parts of writing I described above and analyze them separately (that is, Dialogue, Emotion, Action, Character, and Scene Descriptions).

After you have picked the part of writing you plan to

analyze, you then use our numerical technique to divide it into parts.

Let us take a look at, for example, Character Description:

> A tall skinny girl walked in through the barely open door. Her body was hidden under thick clothing and a heavy winter coat but you could see her skinny hands poking out of her sweater like a crayfish out of its shell.

To analyze this passage, you need to divide the paragraph into parts, which is what we call the numerical technique.

> 1.A tall skinny girl
> 2.walked in through the barely open door.
> 3.Her body was hidden under thick clothing
> 4.and a heavy winter coat
> 5.but you could see her skinny hands poking out of her sweater like a crayfish out of its shell.

Now that you have broken the sentence down, you can do a lot with the various parts.

1. Write similar write-ups

For example:

> "A tall skinny girl" you can change to "A short chubby teenager"

2. You could also label the parts and then write similar write-ups.

For example:

> 1.A tall skinny girl (Description)
> 2.walked through the barely open door. (Action)
> 3.Her body was hidden under thick clothing (Description of part)
> 4.and a heavy winter coat (another Description of part)
> 5.but you could see her skinny hands poking out of her sweater like a crayfish out of its shell (simile)

After you have broken it down like this, you can write similar character descriptions by using the same skeleton, that is, Description, Action, Description, Description and Simile.

Or you could jumble them up, say, Action, Description, Simile, and so on.

You can use these guidelines to polish your work and in the process it will make you a better writer.